C000164688

1 MONT

FREE

READING

at

www.ForgottenBooks.com

By purchasing this book you are eligible for one month membership to ForgottenBooks.com, giving you unlimited access to our entire collection of over 1,000,000 titles via our web site and mobile apps.

To claim your free month visit:

www.forgottenbooks.com/free175735

ISBN 978-0-265-24613-9
PIBN 10175735

Forgotten Books is a registered trademark of FB &c Ltd.
Copyright © 2018 FB &c Ltd.
FB &c Ltd, Dalton House, 60 Windsor Avenue, London, SW19 2RR.
Company number 08720141. Registered in England and Wales.

For support please visit www.forgottenbooks.com

THE SHORT COURSE SERIES

THE PSALM OF PSALMS

GENERAL PREFACE

THE title of the present series is a sufficient indication of its purpose. Few preachers, or congregations, will face the long courses of expository lectures which characterised the preaching of the past, but there is a growing conviction on the part of some that an occasional short course, of six or eight connected studies on one definite theme, is a necessity of their mental and ministerial life. It is at this point the projected series would strike in. It would suggest to those who are mapping out a scheme of work for the future a variety of subjects which might possibly be utilised in this way.

The appeal, however, will not be restricted to ministers or preachers. The various volumes will meet the needs of laymen and

ii

General Preface

Sabbath-school teachers who are interested in a scholarly but also practical exposition of Bible history and doctrine. In the hands of office-bearers and mission-workers the "Short Course Series" may easily become one of the most convenient and valuable of Bible helps.

It need scarcely be added that while an effort has been made to secure, as far as possible, a general uniformity in the scope and character of the series, the final responsibility for the special interpretations and opinions introduced into the separate volumes, rests entirely with the individual contributors.

A detailed list of the authors and their subjects will be found at the close of each volume.

The Short Course Series

EDITED BY

Rev. JOHN ADAMS, B.D.

THE
PSALM OF PSALMS

BEING AN EXPOSITION OF THE TWENTY-THIRD PSALM

BY THE

Rev. JAMES STALKER, M.A., D.D.,

PROFESSOR OF CHURCH HISTORY IN THE UNITED FREE COLLEGE
ABERDEEN

NEW YORK

CHARLES SCRIBNER'S SONS

1913

TO

T. O.

CONTENTS

THE Twenty-third Psalm is the nightingale among the Psalms. It is small, of a homely feather, singing shyly out of obscurity; but it has filled the air of the whole world with melodious joy, greater than the heart can conceive. Blessed be the day on which that Psalm was born !

HENRY WARD BEECHER.

INTRODUCTION

INTRODUCTION

THE Decalogue, the Aaronic Blessing and the Twenty-third Psalm in the Old Testament, and the Beatitudes, the Lord's Prayer and the Apostolic Benediction in the New, with perhaps two or three other passages of similar calibre, are the best-known portions of Holy Writ. They were learned by us at a mother's knee, or at least from our earliest instructors; and they are all of sufficient substance to stand constant repetition, as solid gold is only brightened by frequent rubbing. To generations and centuries of men such scriptures have ministered "doctrine, reproof, correction, instruction in righteousness"; and, though they are the earliest efforts of memory, they will reward the maturest ponderings of the human mind. The Twenty-third Psalm, in particular, ever since it sprang into existence from the inspired genius of its author, has served to express the experience of the pious ; and the modern man can measure his own progress and attainment by the extent to which he can make its sentiments his own. Not only, however, will the venerable words measure attainment, but they will stimulate it and awaken higher aspiration. Hence the psalm is worthy to be studied verse by verse and line by line.

I. Authorship.

There was a time, not very long ago, when any psalm might be quoted as a psalm of David. We have now reached a stage when it would be denied by experts of a certain class that even a single psalm can be proved to have proceeded from the Bard of Bethlehem. The one extreme is, however, as untenable as the other. When the controversy about such subjects first broke out in the Church with which I am connected, I remember a minister of saintliness and learn-

Introduction

ing declaring that for him the Fifty-first Psalm would lose all its virtue if it were not from the pen of David; and some may be inclined to say the same about this Twenty-third Psalm. I should not like to say this peremptorily about any piece in the Psalter; and in general I like to think of the Psalms as proceeding from a large number and variety of voices spread at intervals over the pre-Christian centuries. But, on the other hand, when the attribution of a psalm to some known personage, or its connection with some recorded event, throws light on the whole composition, and is not inconsistent with anything in the text, it seems to me to be extinguishing the light not to take advantage of this circumstance.

Now, the reasons for believing this Twenty-third Psalm to be a legacy bequeathed to the people of God by King David are very strong indeed, and the assumption that he is the author throws light on every verse.

First, it lies on the surface that the relation of God to His people is here compared to the relation of a shepherd to his sheep;

The Psalm of Psalms

and of this David could speak from experience, as he had been a shepherd. Indeed, the suggestion has not infrequently been made that he may have composed this lyric whilst as a ruddy youth he was watching his flocks on the pastures of his father Jesse. On the other hand, however, it has been observed with truth that the experience here described is not that of a stripling or beginner, but of one mature in the life divine, who has had experience of all forms of guidance, in vicissitude as well as rest, in gloom as well as sunshine. But, even if the psalm was composed in old age or at least maturity, as it probably was, the sweet singer could make use of the experiences of his youth, which he could not have forgotten. At that time he had been a model shepherd, loving his flock and loved by them ; and in the psalm the entire life of a sheep under a good shepherd is employed as an image or parable of a human life led under the guidance and protection of God.

But it may not have been noted by some readers, often as they have read and sung

6

Introduction

this psalm, that, in the second half of it, we are away from the image of the sheep altogether, and that another image is being developed. When, at v. 5, it is said, " Thou preparest a table before me in the presence of mine enemies ; Thou anointest my head with oil ; my cup runneth over," it is obvious that the words are put not into the mouth of a sheep, but into that of a guest, and that the person addressed is no longer conceived of as a shepherd, but as a host or entertainer. The table spread, the head anointed, the cup full to overflowing are obvious features of a banquet ; and the idea is, that he who has God for his friend enjoys a continual feast, where everything is in abundance and everything is of the best. The same cheerful image is kept up in the closing verse—" Goodness and mercy shall follow me all the days of my life ; and I will dwell in the house of the Lord for ever." The favourite is not only to be a guest, but one who abides in the house for ever—that is, a son.

The point to be observed is, that this

second image agrees, as well as does the first, with the experience of David. If, during the first half of his life, he was a shepherd, he was, during the second half, a king ; and one of the duties of a king is hospitality. Indeed, this trait is mentioned again and again in the history as characteristic of David's mature life ; and what a fascination he exercised as a host may be inferred from the offer of two of his braves to risk their lives in order to procure what he wanted, when he expressed a desire to taste a draught of water from the Well of Bethlehem. To his guests he could supply not only the good things of the table, but, with his musical gifts, the feast of reason and the flow of soul. If David was a model shepherd at one period of life, he was a model entertainer at another ; and this experience also supplied him with the means of illustrating both the behaviour of God to men and the attitude of men to God.

We shall see afterwards why it was that David found the image of the ʰepherd insufficient, and had to add that of the royal

Introduction

entertainer. But, in the meantime, we perceive how natural it was that he should employ both figures of speech. I do not deny that another poet might have hit upon the same combination without having had either experience in his own case. But to have had the double experience in the same lifetime must have been a very rare thing. It certainly adds to the value of the psalm if we assume that the sweet singer was speaking from experience in both the beginning and the end of it. There is a life-likeness which supports this view ; and, though it would be of no use to affirm dogmatically the Davidic authorship, we shall assume this throughout.

II. APPLICATION.

An eccentric professor, under whom I studied at college, used to say that the most important word in a text may be the one after the last ; and it is certainly true that the message of no Old Testament passage is exhausted when it has been interpreted by the mere analysis of the words and their applica-

The Psalm of Psalms

tion to the original situation. The first duty of an interpreter is to find out what the writer meant to convey at the moment when he wrote ; but the words may suggest far more to a Christian reader. Of this a remarkable instance has often struck me : in the Thirty-first Psalm a saintly singer says, "Into thine hand I commit my spirit" ; but our Saviour, in quoting the words on the cross, prefaced them with the word "Father," thus placing on them His own distinctive signature ; and St. Stephen, in adopting them as his dying words, actually addressed them to the Saviour Himself, saying, "Lord Jesus, receive my spirit." This indicates how wide may be the scope of legitimate Christian application.

The principle applies to our Psalm also, which is a fine example of how the beautiful and profound passages of the Old Testament become far more beautiful and far more profound when read in the light of the New.

The image of the Good Shepherd, applied in the Old Testament to God, is applied in the New Testament to Christ ; it is especially

Introduction

applied by Jesus to Himself, as when He says, "The good shepherd giveth his life for the sheep." David might have introduced this feature into the Twenty-third Psalm; because, as we know from the account he gave of himself at his first interview with King Saul, there were more occasions than one when he risked his life for the flock. He omitted it; but the Son of David could not omit it, because this was to be His most characteristic act; "for the Son of man came not to be ministered unto but to minister, and to give his life a ransom for many." Some in our day are teaching that the supreme and final message of Jesus was trust in Providence—faith that the divine will, whatever it may be, is best. That is a priceless lesson; but it had been amply taught long before the Incarnation. Jesus rejoiced in it, and repeated it; but it was not His last word; it is not likely that He stopped short at such truth as had already been perfectly uttered by King David.

The other image of the Twenty-third Psalm is the Royal Entertainer; and this,

The Psalm of Psalms

too, recurs in the words of Jesus, but with a deepened meaning. He frequently, in His parables, compared the Gospel to a feast. Even in this world Christianity turns human life into a festival, and in the world to come the life of the blessed will be the Marriage Supper of the Lamb. For Christ brought life and immortality to light. He spoke of the world unseen as of a place native and familiar; and His own Resurrection and Ascension opened the gates of heaven to all believers. Thus what the Old Testament saints only groped after is now for us a sure possession.

Closely allied to this image is the institution of the Lord's Supper, in which Christ goes down through all the centuries, to the end of time, in the character of Royal Entertainer, with these words encircling His figure, "This Man receiveth sinners and eateth with them." Of this, Sir H. W. Baker has taken advantage in the eucharistic hymn, "The King of love my shepherd is," which is a rendering, verse by verse, of our Psalm, with only a Christian touch added

Introduction

here and there. Hardly, indeed, were even these changes necessary ; for, in its naked simplicity, the Twenty-third Psalm gives such adequate expression to Christian feeling, in even its most intimate moments, that it might compete with the Hundred-and-third or the Hundred-and-sixteenth for the title of the Psalm for the Communion Table.

THE GOOD SHEPHERD

THE GOOD SHEPHERD

VERSE FIRST.

"The Lord is my shepherd;
I shall not want."

THE handling of the material in this psalm is very artistic. The primary idea is expressed in the opening words, "The Lord is my Shepherd"; and then, to the end of v. 4, follow inferences from it, mentioning in detail the different things which one who is a good shepherd will do. Of these inferences the first is included in this first verse, "I shall not want." This is the sole negative inference; those that follow are positive.

1. A PROFITABLE PRACTICE.

Not long ago, on opening a new book—a translation from the Dutch—on the Lord's

The Psalm of Psalms

Parables, I was struck with the way in which the subject was divided. First were discussed the parables taken from agriculture, of which there were said to be seven ; then those taken from the work of the vinedresser, of which there were six ; then those taken from the work of the shepherd ; then those from the industry of the fisherman ; and so on.

It brought home to me more distinctly than I had ever observed before, how the common life of Palestine was all swept, for purposes of illustration, into the teaching of Christ—with what an observant and sympathetic eye He had looked upon the common occupations of men, and how suggestive they had been to Him of spiritual analogies.

I suppose, the four occupations to which I have referred were the most common in Palestine. There was, first, agriculture : this was the basis of existence, and in it the body of the people were employed. Then there was the occupation of the vinedresser : every sunny hillside was covered with vineyards, and at the time of the vintage the whole land was filled with the songs of those who gathered and those who trod the grapes. Then there was the occupation of the shepherd : the hills which were not suitable for the cultivation of the vine were clothed with flocks ; and every village had its droves of great and small cattle, which were led out to the pastures every evening. Then there was the labour of the fisherman, which Jesus could not possibly omit, because it was so conspicuous in the part of the country in which the principal scene of His ministry lay.

It was not only, however, nor was it first by Him that these features of common life in the Holy Land were beautifully described and used as vehicles for conveying spiritual truth. In both the poetical and prophetical parts of the Old Testament we find the same practice in full operation. How often, for example, in the Psalms and the Prophets, are the people of God compared to a vine, of which God is the husbandman ; and every single step in the history of the vineyard, from the time it is cleared of stones and fenced in from the surrounding waste on to

The Psalm of Psalms

the point where the wine is in the cup and at the owner's lips, is made use of to illustrate some aspect or other of divine truth. Still more common, if possible, is the use for the same purpose made of the shepherd's calling. As early as the age of the patriarchs, God is called the Shepherd of Israel ; and in a hundred different forms subsequently this thought recurs, every phase and incident of the life of the shepherd and the life-history of the sheep being turned to account, as in the unspeakably beautiful words of Isaiah, "He shall feed His flock like a shepherd ; He shall gather the lambs with His arm and carry them in His bosom, and shall gently lead those that are with young."

Here, then, we see a distinct and prevalent habit of the religious mind. The inspired teachers perceived in the common occupations of daily life innumerable hints and suggestions of heavenly truths, and they taught those who received their teaching to brood upon these analogies as they engaged in their ordinary occupations.

The Good Shepherd

Now this is a precious habit; and we also —both those who teach and those who are taught—ought to cultivate it. The aspect of our modern life is, indeed, very different from that ancient one. Though we still have in our population the agriculturist, the shepherd, and the fisherman, we are not an agricultural but a commercial people, and we have a vast number of other occupations. Some of these may not be so poetical or suggestive as the occupations of a simple open-air existence. But many of them— such as the calling of the builder, the banker, the manufacturer, the engineer—are pregnant with instructive and impressive suggestions; and there is no occupation which is altogether unable to yield such nutrition to the brooding mind.

Existence is ennobled when, besides the prose of mere loss and gain, its occupations thus whisper to the heart the poetry of spiritual suggestion; and our modern world would be a far happier place if it had poets who could thus interpret the hidden meaning of common things. It is not, indeed, destitute of these ; but they are required in far greater numbers. I like to think of the poets who are still to be. There are Homers and Shakspeares, Miltons and Burnses, still to be born. The generations of the future will read glorious books which we have never seen, and be inspired with songs, full of melody and joy, which our ears have never heard. What these strains of the future will be we can only guess ; but no office of poetry is so valuable as that of dignifying common life by revealing the filaments by which it is connected with an ideal region—the life spiritual and eternal.

Meanwhile, let us be thankful for this, that every man is in some degree a poet. There is an inarticulate poetry which never goes into words or books, but warms, delights and refines the soul in which it simmers. The apprentice has it who, as he measures a yard of ribbon or sells a pound of sugar, is thinking of how trade unites the races of the world and makes all men servants one of another ; the working man has it who, as he chisels a stone for its place in a building, is thinking how the providence of daily experience is shaping himself for a place in the temple of God ; the servant has it who, as she sweeps a room or scours a vessel, is praying that her heart may be a clean abode for the habitation of God's Spirit. Even the scavenger may be rapt by it out of the gutter, where he is employed, up to the heavenly places ; and, if he is, then in the genuine attributes of manhood he far excels the gentleman in broadcloth who may despise him, as he passes, if the soul of the latter does not soar above pounds, shillings and pence.

2. A Fruitful Analogy.

Although all lawful occupations will yield some analogies to divine truth, there are, of course, certain which are more fertile in this respect than others ; and the religious language of all ages seems to prove that in the occupation of the shepherd such analogies are particularly obvious.

Perhaps, indeed, this was more the case in the East than it is in this country. The

The Psalm of Psalms

shepherds of our border hills are a superior class of men, and their care for the flocks entrusted to them is exemplary, but the Oriental shepherd was brought much nearer his sheep, and his affection for them was more peculiar. By two circumstances especially was this demonstrated—the one, the well-known fact that, instead of driving his sheep, the Oriental shepherd goes before them, whilst they follow; the other, the fact that he not only knows his own sheep by head-mark, as, I suppose, our shepherds also do, but calls each of them by its own name. In our mountains it is not unusual to see sheep on the hillside with no shepherd in sight, especially where there is an enclosing wall or fence, the presence of a shepherd being not always necessary. But in the East, sheep are never seen without the shepherd. In Eastern fields there are no fences, and danger is never far off: the wolf or the panther may be prowling about, or the robber from the desert may be on the watch. Our shepherds go out in the morning with nothing but plaid and staff; but in the East, even at the present day, the shepherd goes afield armed to the teeth with gun, sword, or other weapons; and it is no very unusual incident for a shepherd actually to sacrifice his life for his flock.

Of course all shepherds are not alike faithful or affectionate; but we can easily believe that David was an ideal shepherd. We remember how he slew the lion and the bear by which his flock had been attacked; and, even if we were unacquainted with these incidents, we could imagine how his generous heart would have gone out to the creatures under his charge, and how his courage would have prompted him to sacrifice himself for their protection. We may be certain of this, too, that the intensity of David's fidelity became to him an interpreter of God's faithfulness to those over whose welfare He had pledged Himself to watch. In the same way, it is the man who is himself the most affectionate and loyal father who best knows what is meant by the fatherhood of God. And in general, we may lay down the rule that it is the man who

The Psalm of Psalms

loves his occupation and is doing his daily work with all his might who will best perceive the divine lessons it is fitted to teach.

The shepherd's care of his sheep begins with the most elementary wants of existence, but it mounts up, through successive stages of attention and kindness, till it may culminate in the sacrifice of his life on their behalf. At every step this has its counterpart in God : we are dependent on Him for our daily bread ; and upon numerous steps the tale of His grace has to be told, till we come to the astounding fact that " the Good Shepherd giveth His life for the sheep."

Thus the relation of God to the soul of man is attractively and suggestively set forth by the relation of the shepherd to the sheep. Perhaps on the opposite side—the relation of the soul to God, which is the other half of religion—the analogy is not so serviceable.

Here also, indeed, there are pathetic hints of the truth. The sheep has a tendency to stray and lose itself. So all we, like sheep, have gone astray ; we have turned every one to his own way.

The Good Shepherd

There are some animals, such as the dog, which, though lost, have a remarkable faculty of finding their way home. The sheep is, however, I should think, deficient in this kind of intelligence : if lost, it has no instinct for finding itself again. Here also, it may be said, the analogy holds. When man lost God, he would never of his own accord have come home. God had to come after him.

But none of the righteous ever knew
　　How deep were the waters crossed,
Or how dark was the night that the Lord passed through,
　　Ere He found the sheep that was lost.
　　　　Out in the desert He heard its cry,
　　　　Sick and helpless and ready to die.

Lord, whence are those blood drops all the way
　　That mark out the mountain track?
They were shed for one who had gone astray,
　　Ere the Shepherd could bring him back.
　　　　Lord, whence are Thy hands so rent and torn?
　　　　They were pierced tonight by many a thorn.

As we say this of the human race as a whole, so of every individual soul it may be said that it never could and never would have returned of its own accord. God has to send forth His Spirit to seek, to strive and persuade. "No man can come unto Me, except the Father, which hath sent Me, draw him."

But the responsibility of man to yield to these strivings of God's Spirit, and his freedom either to continue in sin or to come home to God, are very imperfectly represented by anything in the case of the sheep. So especially is the choice by which we turn away from all other masters and acknowledge God as our own God—the most important moment of religion on man's side.

There are also other points at which the relation of the sheep to the shepherd does not express very well the relation of the soul to God. But of nearly all analogies the same is true—they illustrate only a limited number of points, while at other points they break down. And our wisdom is to bring into the light those aspects of the truth which an image fairly illustrates, letting the others fall into the background. The image of the shepherd and the sheep illustrates so many points so well that there is no need of forcing it to do work for which it was not intended.

3. A Golden Promise.

The first inference drawn from the great statement "The Lord is my shepherd," is, "I shall not want." This is merely negative; yet how priceless it is! In the strength of such a promise a pilgrim might almost travel the whole way.

Many people are haunted all their days with the fear of want; and, although they have no real trouble today, they are continually borrowing it from tomorrow, and so allowing their entire existence to be overshadowed. Many even of the young are haunted with the dread that, however well they may live and however honestly they may work, the world may have no room for them and may not even afford them their daily bread. But this is a morbid and unbelieving state of mind, and not in accordance with facts. Society is always in need of upright men and women and honest workers, and does not grudge them their wages. The fact that we have been brought into existence is a proof that we are needed; and the likelihood is strong that a sufficient share of what is required to sustain existence will be ours, if we are willing to do our part to deserve our place. This is the cheerful philosophy of Jesus Himself: "Consider the lilies of the field how they grow: they toil not neither do they spin; and yet I say unto you that Solomon in all his glory was not arrayed like one of these. Wherefore, if God so clothe the grass of the field, which today is, and tomorrow is cast into the oven, shall He not much more clothe you, O ye of little faith? Behold the fowls of the air: for they sow not, neither do they reap, nor gather into barns; yet your Heavenly Father feedeth them. Are ye not much better than they?"

Can we say, then, that poverty never can overtake the godly? I once heard the late Mr. Spurgeon, in his own church, read a psalm in which this verse occurs: "I have been young and now am old, yet have I not seen the righteous forsaken, or his seed begging bread." After reading the verse, he paused and remarked, "David, being a king, may never have seen this spectacle; but I, being a minister and better acquainted with poor people, have seen it often." That was a very bold statement. Let me quote to you another of an opposite tenor. I was once walking through a poorhouse with the manager, a wise and kindly man, and, being pained with what I had seen, I said to him, "Tell me, now, what proportion of the inmates of this house have been well-doing people, and have been brought here by no fault of their own." "Well," he answered, "I know them all well, and I am acquainted with their histories, and, I am sorry to say, there is not a single one of the sort you have indicated."

These are widely discrepant statements, and perhaps both of them might mislead. An enormous quantity of abject poverty—probably a far larger proportion of it than in the present temper of the public mind would be readily believed—is due to vice; in our own society it is especially due to drunkenness. Character and well-doing, on the contrary, usually lift at least to the level of honest poverty, with which the dignity and sunshine of life are not incompatible. Besides, where character and well-doing are, there is the power to rally against misfortune : poverty may crush for a time, but the God-fearing spirit will rise above it, and life will improve as it proceeds. On the other hand, however, modern society is so complex that many have to suffer for the wrong-doing of others ; and it would be blind and cruel to doubt that sometimes the deserving may sink into destitution, and that in the almshouse, and even the poorhouse, there are saints of God.

What do these exceptional cases prove ? Do they prove that sometimes God's promise fails ? If we look to Jesus, we shall understand the mystery. Though He spoke so cheerfully of God's good providence, yet He had to say Himself, " Foxes have holes, and the birds of the air have nests ; but the Son of man hath not where

The Good Shepherd

to lay His head "; and He died forsaken and outcast. Still, through all, He kept His eye fixed on God and never doubted that out of the darkest misfortune He would cause to be born a higher good. Nor was He disappointed; for out of His bitter shame has come His exaltation, and out of His loss and suffering the salvation of the world. So out of the mysteries of God's providence will there be born glorious surprises for His other children also. His resources are not exhausted in this life: even after death He can still justify Himself. If God causes any of His saints to want one thing, it is only that He may give a better.

> Deep in unfathomable mines
>   Of never-failing skill
> He treasures up His bright designs
>   And works His sovereign will.
>
> Ye fearful saints, fresh courage take,
>   The clouds ye so much dread
> Are big with mercy and will break
>   In blessing on your head.

REST

35

REST

"He maketh me to lie down in green pastures;
He leadeth me beside the still waters."

After, in verse 1, announcing the theme of
the Psalm to be a comparison between the
Lord's care of His people and a shepherd's
care of his flock, the sacred poet goes on to
illustrate the different kinds of fortune
through which human beings pass and in
which they experience the divine care and
sympathy; and each of these is illustrated
by a corresponding situation in the history
of the sheep under the shepherd's guidance.
Life is full of transitions and vicissitudes;
sometimes it is in sunshine, sometimes in
shadow; sometimes it is on the heights,
sometimes in the depths; but in every one

of its varying phases God is still at hand, watching over His own and doing all things well.

The imperial singer begins with prosperity, of which he gives this picture taken from the pastoral life : " He maketh me lie down in green pastures ; He leadeth me beside the still waters." This is, as someone has said, the most complete picture of happiness that ever was or can be drawn.

But why does he begin with this ? Why does he describe the experience of pro- sperity before that of adversity ? Someone has answered, Because it is the commoner state. The lot of God's people is, on the whole, one of happiness. Seasons of suffer- ing there are, indeed ; and they are vividly remembered—just as an obstruction in a river makes a great show and causes a great noise ; but the life of the Christian is for the most part like a tranquil stream, which flows deep and does not invite attention.

Lord Bacon has the aphorism that, while prosperity was the promise of the Old Testa- ment, adversity is the blessing of the New.

Rest

But is this true? There are doubtless many weighty words of the New Testament which speak of the cross which Christians must bear and the persecutions they may have to suffer: "Whosoever doth not bear his cross and come after Me, cannot be My disciple"; "Marvel not if the world hateth you; ye know that it hated Me before it hated you." Such words abound among the sayings of our Lord and His apostles. But they do not stand alone; and, when quoted alone, they convey a misleading impression. What said the Master Himself? "Verily, I say unto you, there is no man who hath left house, or brethren or sisters, or father or mother, or wife or children, for My sake and the gospel's, but he shall receive a hundredfold more in this time, houses, and brethren and sisters, and mothers and children, and lands, with persecutions; and in the world to come eternal life." Similarly an apostle declares: "Godliness is profitable unto all things, having promise of the life which now is and of that which is to come." The New Testament is not a sadder book

than the Old; on the contrary, it is far more
sunny and melodious; and this is not only
because the misery of the present life is to
be compensated by the felicity of the life to
come, but this life itself is a happy one.

> The world's no blank to us
> Nor blot; it means intensely, and means good.

1. Temporal Prosperity.

This is true in regard to temporal prosperity. The tendency of things is to throw
into the lap of God's people the best blessings
even of this earthly life.

What are these? Health is one of them.
This is a fundamental blessing, on which
many more depend. All sights look dreary
when seen through the jaundiced eyes of
disease, and all pleasures are tasteless when
they touch an unhealthy palate. But, when
the blood is flowing limpidly through the
veins and the brain is fresh and unclogged,
God's glorious world, with its sights and
sounds, gratifies the senses and awakens
desire; things have their natural taste, and

the simple elements of life are enough to satisfy without the condiment of artificial pleasure. Now, health is most likely to be the heritage of those who obey the laws of God. By the excesses of an ungoverned youth, many are sowing in their own bodily constitution the seeds of a debilitated manhood and an early death. They are burning out in themselves the very sense for natural pleasure and creating the necessity for artificial stimulation, which loses its effect the oftener it is applied. Those who listen to the voice of God and follow the path of virtue may be scoffed at, because, during the opportunities of youth, they do not follow the hot and highly seasoned pleasures which others pursue; but their enjoyment lasts longer, and at the period when others are falling bankrupt they are coming into the full enjoyment of their heritage.

Another of the best blessings of life is love. It is by the heart mainly that human beings are made blessed or miserable; and it is a notable evidence of the equality of nature that love is restricted to no class or grade of culture or fortune. The poorest may feel the glow of pure affection and be loyal to the vows of friendship. Love culminates in the home, and he who possesses a happy home, where the hunger of the heart is satisfied and the voice of innocent mirth is heard, has not missed the best which this earthly life can yield. But to whom does the blessing of love belong? Many prostitute the name by applying it to indulgences which make true love impossible; for impurity "hardens a' within and petrifies the feeling." He who wastes his youth is robbing himself beforehand of the power of giving to a pure woman, should he be so fortunate as to win the love of such a one, heart for heart; he is robbing himself beforehand of the power of looking in his children's faces unashamed; and it is more than possible that his offspring may have to pay with lives of misery the penalty of his sin. If the glory of friendship is that each friend knows the other to be absolutely transparent and true; if love is the exchange of hearts which have been kept for one another unspent and undefiled ; if home is, as has been said, the one bit of Paradise left in a fallen world ; then is the gift of love, in all its perfection and splendour, peculiarly the heritage of those who have taken God's law and Christ's will as the rule of their life.

Another of these blessings is business success. Of this, indeed, too high an estimate may be formed. In a business community financial success is deified, and multitudes, though perhaps they are hardly aware of the fact, worship no other God. On the other hand, it is possible to depreciate success too much. Business is, by the allotment of Providence, that to which the majority have to devote the most of their time and the best of their strength. To depreciate it, therefore, as if it did not matter whether or not a man did it with all his might, is only to confuse the mind and perplex the conscience. Business is a providential school of virtue, in which manhood is developed and the natural powers are exercised, and success is, as a rule, the evidence that we have not been faithless or laggard scholars. To whom does success fall? Some would answer, To the selfish and unscrupulous — to those who mind Number One and never hesitate to fling down or trample on a competitor, and to those who, when occasion requires, can, without flinching, stoop to falsehood. Alas, there are too many facts which might be adduced in support of such a view of business. Yet it is a partial view, and there is a vast body of facts on the opposite side. Unscrupulousness sometimes succeeds, and often quite eclipses honesty in the rapidity with which it reaches the goal ; but its prosperity is frequently short-lived and its hollowness is exposed at last. Character tells in business. It may not do so today, but it will tomorrow. "The meek," said our Lord, "shall inherit the earth." It seems a paradox ; for are not the meek thrust aside and trampled in an age like ours by the pushing and self-assertive? Yes, they are ; but their turn comes. The gilt of pretentious talents is soon rubbed off, and then what it has covered looks shabby ; but the solid gold of character shines more and more the longer it is rubbed, and in due time its value is acknowledged. There are those who will tell you that the Decalogue is abrogated in the business-world, and that the Sermon on the Mount, though beautiful to read in a castle-in-the-air, has no meaning in the market-place. But the Decalogue and the Sermon on the Mount have a way of living on, whilst their critics pass away. Some men also venture to take these rules into the market-place; and the God who made the Decalogue and the Christ who preached the Sermon do not allow them to be put to shame.

Some possess all these blessings of the earthly life which I have mentioned and many more besides. They have the gift of health; they have known love in all its sweet, pure forms; their friends are warm and true; their home is a scene of tranquillity in which they find refuge from the turmoils of the world; their children are affectionate and well-doing; and God has so blessed the labour of their hands that they have never lacked bread to eat or raiment to put on.

The Psalm of Psalms

The lines have fallen unto them in pleasant places. Theirs is the condition our text describes: "He maketh me to lie down in green pastures; He leadeth me beside the still waters."

God has given these gifts. With what effect on the relation between your soul and Him? It is an astonishing thing how often in Scripture spiritual improvement is ascribed to affliction and misfortune. "Before I was afflicted I went astray, but now I have learned thy law." "Whom the Lord loveth He chasteneth, and scourgeth every son whom He receiveth." In experience, too, we find that religious improvement is closely connected with suffering. Hundreds of times we have heard of sinners being converted by a severe illness or a great bereavement; but who ever heard of a man being converted by a windfall of good fortune? It is not creditable that we are thus dependent for our religion on the withdrawal of temporal blessings and so little affected by the possession of them.

I do not, however, believe that loss alone

sanctifies. Happiness does so too. A heart made happy by pure love is not far from the kingdom of God. The coming of a child into a family sometimes opens the door for Christ. Prosperity in business breeds liberality in giving. Only, such virtues ought far oftener to spring from God's goodness. Many of us, if we would only, in a sequestered hour, look back on the way we have been led, and look round on the ample and sunny heritage in which God has placed us, could see a thousand reasons for clinging with boundless gratitude and loyalty to Him and to the kingdom of His Son.

2. SPIRITUAL PROSPERITY.

When, however, the psalmist says, "Thou makest me to lie down in green pastures, Thou leadest me beside the still waters," he cannot be referring to temporal blessings alone : this is also a description of the life spiritual.

Valuable as temporal blessings are, a Christian must hold them with a light hand

and be ready to sacrifice them for the sake of the integrity of the life within. Christians have, in fact, often thus sacrificed every worldly possession and every worldly prospect and laid down even life itself. A Christian lives in the world like other men ; he attends to business and derives profits from it ; he enjoys the delight of friendship and the comfort of home ; yet he has, at the same time, a life which ordinary men of the world have not—a life remote and solitary, hid with Christ in God. A portion of human nature which in other men is dormant has in him been awakened ; he is in living intercourse with the world unseen ; the powers of his spirit are in activity, going forth towards their proper objects—to God, to Christ, to truth, to eternity.

Now this spiritual life, taken as a whole, is a supremely happy life, and brings fresh currents of joy into the being. So voluminous are these that they are able to make up for the loss of ordinary temporal comforts and enjoyments. Look at a man like St. Paul. He lost much by being a Christian ;

he suffered much; but was he an unhappy man? On the contrary, an exuberant life throbs in all his movements, and an irrepressible joy rings, like a peal of bells, in all his writings.

What are the enjoyments of this hidden life?

One of them is love. I have already spoken of the deep pleasure of ordinary human love. But the heart of man has been fashioned with the capacity for a love profounder and nobler than the love of friend or father, wife or child. We are capable of loving God and His Son Jesus Christ. In many hearts this is a capacity and nothing more, just as other forms of affection may never reach their realisation. Many do not love God; they do not love the Saviour. But where this divine affection is awakened into activity, it is not only the most sacred and influential, but also the most delightful and satisfying emotion which the heart can know. If to love another human being, and to know that you are held dear by another human heart, be one of the crowning experiences of life, what must it be to love God and to know that you are held dear in the heart of Christ?

It is almost choosing at random from a wide field of selection, when I mention as another of the enjoyments of the interior life delight in the Word of God. I mention this because the words of our text have often been applied to it. When enjoying revealed truth, Christians often speak of themselves as lying down in green pastures and being led beside still waters. Thus one says, "What are these green pastures but the Scriptures of truth—always fresh, always rich, and never exhausted? Sweet and full are the doctrines of the gospel, fit food for souls, as tender grass is nutriment for sheep. When by faith we are enabled to find rest in the promises, we are like the sheep that lie down in the midst of pastures ; we find at the same moment both provender and peace, rest and refreshment, serenity and satisfaction." There are those who read the Bible and enjoy it for its literary qualities alone ; and, indeed, by its profundity of thought and beauty of diction, it is placed at the head of all literature. But the delight of a spiritual mind in it is deeper : the Bible is one of the principal means through which it maintains its connexion and intercourse with the divine heart which it loves.

Let me name but one more enjoyment of the hidden life—the bliss of doing good. This bliss is not, indeed, the exclusive property of the spiritual. There are those who, from natural goodness of heart or the influence of good tradition and training, care continually for the welfare of their neighbours ; and none can do so, whatever be their motives, without having a rich blessing returned into their own bosoms. But the passion of doing good belongs peculiarly to Christians. They have learned it from Christ. Looking on their fellow-men through His eyes, they perceive both their infinite worth and their immeasurable danger. Having received salvation themselves, they feel an instinctive desire to communicate the secret to others. In this work many emotions are stirred, some of them painful and some pleasurable. It is work which is liable to encounter opposition ; and the opposition may wax deadly. But, on the whole, the reward of such work is great. No man ever yet exerted himself for the temporal and eternal welfare of others without being himself enriched. And, when the work is successful, and men and women are saved, and they pour their gratitude on our heads, who can measure the joy ? It is worth living for, to be made the instrumentality through which has been wrought an immortal good.

This is what some would call, not without a touch of contempt, the hedonistic or eudæmonistic aspect of Christianity ; and they would deprecate the emphasizing of this pleasurable element in religion. Better, they would say, emphasize the sober fact that religion is a duty to be done, a yoke to be felt, a cross to bear. I do not, however, think so. Let each side of the truth have its turn. And, after all, Christianity must always be far more a gift from God to man than a gift from man to God.

Rest

It is of the utmost consequence to proclaim and reiterate that the blessedness of man is hidden at the centre of his own being : it lies in the opening up of the hidden world of the spirit, into which Christianity invites him. It is there that man meets God and enters into the fulness of salvation by Jesus Christ. Let no one leave the world without seeing the one vision it contains, or die without ever having lived.

DISCIPLINE

DISCIPLINE

VERSE THIRD.

"He restoreth my soul;
He leadeth me in the paths of righteousness for His
name's sake."

IN the Twenty-third Psalm the different kinds
of experience through which the people of
God pass are set forth by different incidents
in the life of a flock of sheep. The point
is, that the shepherd is always present and
watchful, consulting for the welfare of the
creatures committed to his care; and in the
same way God is with His people in every
variety of fortune, seeing to it that all things
work together for their good. Verse 2 is a
perfect picture of prosperity; but verse 3 is
a picture of adversity.

The Psalm of Psalms

1. The Fainting-fits of the Soul.

"He restoreth my soul," says the sacred singer. But this implies that the soul is in need of restoration. The picture is that of a sheep which, through heat and fatigue, has fainted away, or is on the point of breathing out its life; but the good shepherd, by administering a restorative in the nick of time, brings back the departing breath. Here we have a totally different picture from that of verse 2. There the sheep was in green pastures; all was sunshine and happiness; life was enjoyable and abundant. But here life is at the lowest ebb; and the sheep has fainted away.

There are such contrasts in experience. Life has its sunshine, but it has also its shadow. There are days of prosperity, when the tides swell the channel of life from bank to brae; but there are also times of adversity, when the pulse of life is low and hope has almost died out of the heart.

This is the case even in the Christian life. On the whole, it is a life of joy—it is the

58

Discipline

happiest of all lives—yet it has its seasons of faintness and despair, when the cordials and restoratives of the Good Shepherd are required.

What are the reasons for these fainting times ?

First of all, a Christian is exposed, like other men, to the misfortunes and calamities of the human lot. There is a passage of Scripture which says that God maketh His sun to rise on the evil and on the good, and sendeth His rain on the just and unjust : there are certain common blessings in which all participate, whatever be their character. But the converse is also true, that there are common misfortunes from which none escape, be their character what it may. The lightning strikes the roof of sinner and saint indiscriminately ; a bad harvest destroys the crops of good and bad alike ; bad times blight the business of the honest as well as of the dishonest ; illness and death are incident to all the children of men. At many points, indeed, godliness will supply alleviations of even such common calamities : when an epidemic is raging, the steady man's chances of recovery are much greater than those of him who has wasted his constitution by dissipation; and, in times when trade fails, the industrious and saving have generally something to fall back on, whereas the reckless, who live from hand to mouth, are thrown on the rocks at once. Still there is in this world a mysterious body of evil from which none can altogether escape. "Man is born to trouble as the sparks fly upwards," and, the more complicated life becomes, through the crowding of population, the more is the individual exposed to suffering for which he is not directly responsible.

Further, however, Christians are exposed to suffering through the very fact that they are Christians. Christ had to warn His first followers that they would be hated of all men for His sake. "Yea, the time cometh," He said, "when whosoever killeth you will think he doeth God service." In many ages this has been literally fulfilled, as is proved by the religious persecutions of ancient and modern times. Nor has the offence of the

Discipline

cross ever ceased. Public persecution has, indeed, ceased, but private persecution still continues; and it is sometimes harder to bear. The natural heart is still unchanged; and it resents the disturbance to its self-complacency caused by the presence and the criticism of the followers of Jesus. In the archives of the Church we have our books of martyrs, and these are by no means all written yet; but the unwritten persecutions are infinitely vaster in their proportions, and they form one of the causes from which the flock of God faints.

There are, however, deeper causes still. The Christian life has its own special pains and secret crosses. A Christian is a man who has seen an ideal: Christ is his ideal, and the life of Christ is the model with which he is always comparing his own. This breeds a divine discontent; he despises himself; he is often in despair because he has fallen beneath what he ought to be. Perhaps he has been on the heights of communion, inspiration and holiness; but the tides of the Spirit recede, the heart grows cold, indifference comes on, iniquity prevails against him. Even a St. Paul had to cry out in bitterness of spirit, " Oh, wretched man that I am, who shall deliver me from the body of this death ? "

To mention but one other cause of the fainting-fits of the soul : Christians have on their shoulders and on their hearts the public cause of Christ, and, when it is in difficulties or is threatened with failure, they have to bear the burden and the shame. Sometimes it seems as if at the back of Christianity there were no almighty force ; the world is too strong for it ; ancient forms of wrong cannot be overcome ; and wickedness, enthroned in high places, is scornful and insolent. In such cases the ungodly are always ready to exult and ask, " Where is your God now gone ? " The Christian may feel in his own heart that his prayers are not being answered ; perhaps someone near and dear to him is under the power of a vice from which even religion seems unable to deliver him ; and the heart faints with the strain of unceasing shame and long delay.

Discipline

2. THE RESTORATIVES OF THE GOOD SHEPHERD.

I have described the occasions of depression at length; but the Psalm does not do so. What it says is not, "I have many causes of trouble," but, "He restoreth my soul." It is as if the only element of the time of suffering which was remembered was the deliverance from it.

Man's extremity is God's opportunity. The sympathy, the tenderness, and the loving kindness of God would not be fully known were it not for the days of darkness in which He draws near to succour.

If God is ever certain to be near His saints, it is when they are in trouble. Which of all the sheep in a good shepherd's flock is the most certain to have the shepherd's attention? Is it not the one that is ailing? As soon as the cry of distress is heard from afar, see how the shepherd hastens over flood and scaur, leaving the ninety-and-nine to look after themselves. Of a mother's children, which is the one that receives most assiduity? Is it not the one that is in danger? When a child is laid down with fever or has had an accident, the mother's thoughts are never for a moment out of the room ; the love in her heart increases with the danger, till it becomes painful in its intensity, and she takes no rest till the life is restored. Such human experiences make us acquainted with the heart of God ; for the sparks of affection in our composition have been kindled from the fire of love in His nature. Never is He so near, never is His compassion so melting, as when we need Him most. And, when this is realised, the storm within us is changed into a calm. Any grief is bearable if we are able to say, My Shepherd knows.

But what are the restoratives with which God overcomes the fainting-fits of those who put their trust in Him?

They are numerous, and it would be impossible to specify them all. Sometimes, when adversity has lasted long, He causes it to be followed by a time of prosperity ; and the joy of His goodness is all the greater because of the contrast with preceding suffer-

Discipline

ing. The night may be dark, but the day succeeds the night; the rain may be continuous, and the storm may roar as if it would sweep man with all his works off the face of the earth, but the sunshine succeeds the rain, and calm comes after the storm. In the times of persecution which our forefathers had to endure, being hunted like partridges on the mountains, there came now and then, owing to various causes, longer or shorter periods when the zeal of the persecutor slackened and the persecuted were allowed repose. These pauses were called "blinks," and they were greatly enjoyed. At such times their souls were restored. Even in the lives which are most sorely beset with misfortune there are "blinks"; God knows that the human spirit is not able to bear the unceasing strain of calamity, and He gives these intervals of rest. When one source of comfort or joy is taken away, the vacant place is filled with a new one. Thus, into a home from which someone greatly beloved has been removed there is sent a new child; the bereaved hearts revive to welcome the young life; and the cypresses of the grave are hidden beneath the climbing roses of hope.

Sometimes it turns out that the road of adversity is the pathway to prosperity, and apparent calamity is only the disguise in which good fortune is for a little concealed. One of the most famous men of our century has put it on record that what appeared the misfortunes of his early life turned out in the end to be the steps to influence and renown. Again and again he attempted to find refuge from the stress of circumstances by putting into some little haven of common-place comfort, where he might have lived and died a nonentity; but Providence shut up the way in every case and kept him out on the high seas, where, by battling with the storms, he acquired courage and power, and in due time he came to his kingdom. Providence seems sometimes to delight in steering the course of its favourites to the very verge of ruin, till the heart of the voyager quakes with terror, when suddenly, by a skilful turn of the Pilot's hand, the vessel is guided

into the sunny seas of undreamed-of success ;
and the poor human heart, which was half-
dead with dismay, is filled with laughter and
the tongue with song. If in the spiritual
world there are seasons of dryness and of
decline, when the tree of life appears to
wither, there are also times of revival, when
the breath of spring is in the atmosphere
and the movement of spring in the ground
—the flowers appear on the earth, the time
of the singing of birds is come, and the
voice of the turtle is heard in the land.
Over a congregation, or a city, or a country,
there passes the wind of the Spirit of God ;
religion suddenly becomes real ; the powers
of the world to come can almost be seen and
handled ; and to be alive is a joy. This
may be brought about for the individual
through slight means—by meeting with a
new friend, by the influence of a good
minister, by a little success in winning souls,
by realising some new truth of God's Word,
or the like. The Christian life is a succes-
sion of new beginnings ; and they that wait
on the Lord shall renew their strength.

3. The Best Use of Adversity.

The Psalm directs special attention to one of the uses of adversity in the words, "He leadeth me in the paths of righteousness."

Here the poet is holding fast by his metaphor; because it is a fact that in times of peril and fear the sheep of a flock follow close to the shepherd, and keep in a straight path wherever he may lead them. At other times they can expatiate over the fields and may easily wander; but terror makes them keep their eye on the shepherd and follow him without turning to the right hand or the left.

But how true to human experience also is the statement! Adversity has a great deal to do with sanctification.

For one thing, it makes prayer real. Some of us would, I daresay, confess that we never knew what prayer actually was till we were driven to the throne of grace by a calamity that was brea ing our heart. I remember being in Germany immediately after the Franco-Prussian War; and I was told how, during the anxious months of the

Discipline

war-time, the churches, which usually are so empty in that country, were crowded, every time the doors were opened, with fathers and mothers whose sons were at the front. Prayer in days which are without suffering or change is apt to be only a pious form, of which we are weary ; but, when the heart is dreading some impending calamity or the iron of loss has entered into the soul, the old forms are filled with fresh meaning, and the tides of emotion overflow the forms ; we do not measure the time which we spend on our knees, and the words of prayer pour, new and living, from the heart.

The same might be said of the Bible : we read it with opened eyes when we have suffered. Passages which we have read scores of times without seeing their beauty lay hold of our sympathy. Deep calls unto deep—the experience of the writer finds its echo in our breasts. What Goethe said of poetry is true of Scripture :

> Who never ate his bread in sorrow,
> Who never spent the midnight hours
> Weeping and watching for the morrow,
> He knows you not, ye heavenly powers.

The Psalm of Psalms

Thus by the avenue of prayer and by the avenue of the Word we are brought nigh to God through adversity ; but adversity affects character in many other ways. I have known a Christian who, after years of careful living and useful testimony, fell into a state of carelessness and backsliding. Just at this stage a younger brother of his own came from the country to the city, and took up his abode in the same lodging. The younger had expected to receive from the elder a good example ; but, not receiving it, he fell into evil courses, and the issue was disastrous in the extreme. But it terrified the backsliding brother back to his Lord. Thus are we sometimes taught, by the consequences of backsliding in ourselves or others, how evil and how bitter a thing it is to depart from the living God ; and the immovable firmness with which a man stands in the right path, avoiding the very appearance of evil, may be due to the recollection of a fall and its calamitous consequences.

But, in whatever way adversity may lead us in the paths of righteousness and away from the paths of unrighteousness, this is by far the most blessed effect it can produce ; for to a Christian nothing is so good as holiness and nothing so formidable as sin. We all naturally desire prosperity and seek to avoid adversity ; but well may we say, Welcome adversity, welcome suffering, welcome the chastisements of God, if by these we are led in the paths of righteousness.

4. THE BEST GUARANTEE OF PROSPERITY.

The phrase with which this verse closes is not to be neglected—the phrase, "for His name's sake"—because, though the wording of it is brief, the meaning is profound.

Surely God restores the souls of His sheep and leads them in the paths of righteousness for their sakes. When we are in distress, He pities us ; and pity causes Him to give aid. So, when He is leading us in the paths of righteousness, He is doing us a great kindness ; for there is nothing either so discreditable or so miserable to a child of

God as to be walking in the path of un-righteousness. But the Psalm takes a far bolder line : it says that God must do these things for His own sake.

If we look again at the image of the shepherd, we easily see how just this observation is. A shepherd succours his sheep when they are fainting, and leads them back into the straight path when they have gone astray, for their sake—because he is attached to them—but is not his own character involved in the matter ? Would not the countryside ring with his dishonour if in such circumstances he neglected his sheep and left them to die ? So the honour of God is involved in the welfare of His people. He has undertaken their salvation ; and, having begun the good work, He must complete it. If God's people were uniformly unfortunate, the young and the timid would be terrified away from religion. It brings reproach on the name of God when His professing people become backsliders.

This is a strong argument to use in prayer : we can ask Him to save us from our sins and to make us holy, because nothing reflects such credit on His cause as the consistency of those who have named the name of Christ. Nothing can give us stronger hope in praying for friends or relatives who may have fallen under the power of sin: "Good Shepherd, lead them back to the paths of righteousness for Thine own name's sake." Such a form of prayer will impart dignity also to our own lives. We are too apt to seek deliverance from adversity for our own sakes alone; we wish to be in the sunshine of prosperity simply because it is more pleasant to ourselves. But life ought to have a nobler aim. God's glory ought to be our chief end; and, if man is earnestly seeking to glorify God, God will see to it that he also enjoys Him forever.

IN EXTREMIS

IN EXTREMIS

" Yea, though I walk through the valley of the shadow
of death,
I will fear no evil ; for Thou art with me :
Thy rod and Thy staff, they comfort me."

THERE is some difficulty about the correct
translation of this verse. In ancient Hebrew
manuscripts there were no vowels ; only the
consonants are written, the vowels having to
be supplied by the reader. This sometimes
introduces considerable uncertainty. And in
the present case it depends on the vowel or
vowels supplied by the reader whether the
rendering shall be " the valley of shadows "
or " the valley of the shadow of death."
The latter phrase, even if it be incorrect, is
in some respects an extremely happy one,
and it has obtained so strong a hold in every-

The Psalm of Psalms

day speech that it is neither likely nor desirable that it should be displaced. Yet I am inclined to think that "the valley of shadows" is what the writer intended to say.

It reminds us of a phrase in another famous Psalm, "the valley of Baca," which probably means "Weeping." So the Revised Version renders it :

Passing through the Valley of Weeping, they make it a place of springs ;
Yea, the early rain covereth it with blessings.

"The valley of shadows" and "the valley of weeping" must have the same meaning. They are expressions for a particularly trying portion of that ideal journey which all must travel between the cradle and the grave.

It is more than possible, however, that there may have been some actual place bearing the name of the Valley of Shadows in the scenery from which the imagery of this Psalm is borrowed. Somewhere in the hills of Judah, where David kept his flocks, there was a glen through which, at nightfall, the shepherd boy used to lead home his

sheep. They called it the Valley of Shadows
or the Valley of the Shadow of Death;
because there the darkness fell earlier than
elsewhere, and the gloom of night was
deeper. Its ravines were haunted by wild
beasts; and, as the darkness came on, the
distant howl of wolf or hyæna could be
heard. David could remember how, at such
moments, his sheep huddled closely about
his heels, and he prepared to do battle, if
necessary, for their lives. Since then he had
learned that the life of man has also such
passages; but, as the sheep crept under his
protection, so he had learned where to place
his trust: " Yea, though I walk through the
valley of the shadow of death, I will fear
no evil; for Thou art with me: Thy rod
and Thy staff, they comfort me."

1. THE DARK VALLEY.

The chief objection to the translation,
" the valley of the shadow of death," is that
it tends to make us think too exclusively
of death as the portion of experience here

The Psalm of Psalms

intended. The dark valley may, however, occur at other stages of the journey of life.

It will be remembered where, in the *Pilgrim's Progress*, the Valley of the Shadow of Death comes in. It is not at the end, but in the first half of the pilgrim's journey. In thus locating it Bunyan was taking a justifiable liberty, guided by his personal experience ; and never has the scene itself been more graphically described. You remember that perilous path, with a ditch on one side and a quagmire on the other, so that, "when the pilgrim sought to shun the ditch on the one hand, he was ready to tip over into the mire on the other ; also, when he sought to escape the mire, without great carefulness he would be ready to fall into the ditch." The Valley was dark as pitch, and full of hobgoblins, satyrs and dragons of the pit ; "also he heard doleful voices and rushings to and fro" ; and the path was beset with snares and nets, holes and pitfalls. Under this imagery Bunyan bodies forth the spiritual conflicts and terrors, amounting almost to melancholy madness, with which

80

the earlier stages of his own Christian course were beset, and of which such graphic and moving descriptions are found in his autobiography, *Grace Abounding*. These terrible sufferings were, in large measure, due to a nervous temperament. The elements of his nature were dangerously poised; as was the case in a still more extreme degree with another great Englishman of Christian genius—the poet Cowper. But there are many who, if asked to say what to them had been the valley of the shadow of death, would at once think of the period when they were passing through the conviction of sin, so keen was the pain and so deadly the despair which they then endured.

In the case of others, whose temperament is not so highly strung, the causes are more realistic. While there are some lives which move on equably from beginning to end with the smoothness of a boat on a canal, in most there is considerable vicissitude of joy and sorrow, as in the course of a ship which sails the high seas and has to encounter all kinds of weather; and in most also there occur, at least once or twice, crises and catastrophes, when feeling is put on the utmost strain, and the vital forces seem on the point of being crushed out by overwhelming pressure from without or within. We speak of experiences which can turn a person's hair grey, or out of which people emerge as if they had risen from their graves. It is to such extraordinary crises that the description of the text applies.

They may be due to a thousand different causes. Some of these may be public. A great war, for example, may put an enormous strain on the feelings of the inhabitants of a country : when, for weeks and months, tens of thousands of hearts are on the rack for the news of victory or defeat, and every list of killed and wounded that appears is scanned in feverish terror of seeing the name of husband, son or brother. The passage of a devastating epidemic through a city may have a similar effect : when at every turn in the streets the passing hearse is met, and for months the wings of death seem to be flapping about every house. Sometimes a commercial panic works in the same way: when a great bank shuts its door, whereupon failure follows failure, the gentlewoman and the widow are reduced from affluence to beggary, and no man knows but the next letter he opens may inform him that the blow has fallen on his own home.

The private causes of such sufferings are too numerous to be even hinted at. Who can estimate what a wife suffers when she first perceives that her husband is becoming a victim of drink? An honest man, with a beloved wife and a young family depending on him, who is suddenly deprived of work and sees no prospect of being able to keep the wolf from the door, must sometimes in a few weeks pass through the bitterness of death. When a heart that has trusted another and given its whole happiness into its keeping discovers at the critical moment that it has been deceived, it must appear as if the whole universe were falling and as if mankind were nothing but a lie.

But, whether the sacred poet intended it or not, it is not without significance that this

The Psalm of Psalms

experience has been called the Valley of the Shadow of Death.   Death is for mankind the great Valley of Shadows.   Tens of thousands would say that their bereavements had robbed them of the sap and buoyancy of life and made them old—when the mother sat by the bedside and saw the life ebbing away from the son who was the apple of her eye ; when the husband laid in the grave the half of his life ; when the friend lost the friend whose praise was the chief incentive to high endeavour.   Death to many is an event the very thought of which simply stupefies. The stoppage of work, the interruption of plans, the forced renunciation of pleasures, the separation from the near and dear which it implies, are bewildering and horrifying ; and still worse is the voyage out into the unknown, with the new experiences which may have to be encountered there.   Of all enemies Death is not only the last but the worst.   It was one who knew human nature well that said :

> The weariest and most loathed worldly life
> Which age, want, penury and imprisonment
> Can lay on nature is a Paradise
> To what we fear of death.

84

In Extremis

2. THE PRESENCE OF GOD.

Again the poet is back among the experiences of his early days. As the sheep entered the Valley of the Shadows, fear huddled them close round the shepherd; but through contact with his body they became fearless; his well-known voice soothed them; even the touch of his crook, laid on them to keep them together, filled them with confidence.

It has often been asked what is the difference between the rod and the staff, but no very satisfactory answer has, as far as I am aware, been given. Some have regarded the words as two names for the same thing: but this is unlikely, as it would be a manifest tautology. Although it cannot be proved from the modern 'customs of the East, it is most probable that the ancient shepherd carried with him two instruments of his trade—one rod of lighter make, to be used in dealing with the sheep, and another of heavier weight and shod with iron, for the purpose of dealing with the enemies of

The Psalm of Psalms

the sheep, striking at the lion or the bear which might attack them. At all events, in God there are resources corresponding to both : He has all that is required for both the guidance and the protection of His own.

The peace and contentment of the sheep are not, however, due to the rod and staff, but to the bearer of them. And the secret of the heart's peace is God Himself—"I will fear no evil ; for Thou art with me." It is a universal experience that fear departs when the appropriate person is near on whose love, strength or wisdom we can rely. A child dreads to be alone in an empty house ; but to be there along with its mother makes fear impossible. A boy lost in the crowd cries as if his heart would break ; but, carried through the crowd on his father's shoulder, he is as happy as a king. As the train rushes through the night at the rate of fifty miles an hour, what a panic it would cause if the passengers should learn that no one was on the engine ; but, when they have reason to believe that the engineer is with them, they fear no evil.

In Extremis

The prisoner placed at the bar charged with
a crime of which he knows himself to be
innocent would be lost if left to himself to
unwind the rope which the sophistical skill
of the prosecutor is twisting round his neck ;
but, when he looks at the advocate who is
with him, armed with complete knowledge
of the facts and with brilliant powers of
argument, he is not afraid.

There can be no circumstances in which
God is not with His own. It has been
pointed out that the four verses about the
Good Shepherd in the Twenty-third Psalm
correspond in a remarkable way with four
names of God—verse 1, " The Lord is my
Shepherd, I shall not want," with Jehovah-
jireh, the Lord will provide ; verse 2, " He
maketh me to lie down in green pastures :
He leadeth me beside the still waters," with
Jehovah-shalom, the Lord is our peace ; verse
3, " He restoreth my soul : He leadeth me in
the paths of righteousness for His name's
sake," with Jehovah-tsidkenu, the Lord our
righteousness ; and verse 4, " Yea, though I
walk through the valley of the shadow of

death, I will fear no evil : for Thou art with me ; Thy rod and Thy staff they comfort me," with Jehovah-shammah, the Lord is there.

Jehovah-shammah is one of the watchwords of the spiritual life. Ascend I into heaven, He is there ; descend I into hell, He is there. Be my lot in sunshine or in darkness, in health or in sickness, He is there. When I am on a bed of weakness, when I am drawing my latest breath, and when I stand before the great white throne, still Jehovah-shammah, the Lord will be there ; and I will fear no evil.

This is a secret which thousands of times has transmuted the bed of death from a place of fear and mortal defeat into a scene of victory and transfiguration. This is the secret : "Lo, I am with you alway even to the end of the world. Amen."

THE ROYAL ENTERTAINER

THE ROYAL ENTERTAINER

Verse Fifth.

"Thou preparest a table before me in the presence of
    mine enemies:
Thou anointest mine head with oil;
My cup runneth over."

At the fifth verse, it is manifest, the figure
of speech is changed. Up to this point
every clause has been a picture from the
experience of the sheep; but, when the
singer says, "Thou preparest a table before
me in the presence of mine enemies; thou
anointest mine head with oil; my cup runneth over," it is obvious that the figure of
the sheep and the shepherd is entirely
dropped.

1. The New Figure of Speech.

If at this point the figure of speech is
changed, it is a question what the next
figure is.

The Psalm of Psalms

In a published sermon, characterized by spiritual power and especially by the vividness imparted to the interpretation of the Old Testament by knowledge of the Orient, Principal George Adam Smith takes this verse as a picture of a scene from pastoral life. He thinks the speaker is a fugitive who, having committed some crime, is pursued by the avengers of blood, and has taken refuge in the tent of a shepherd-chief. By Eastern law and custom such a fugitive would be protected with all the resources of the person on whose mercy he had cast himself, and regaled with the best which the encampment could afford. It is a truly tragic picture to see the fugitive there within, protected by the sheikh and feasting on the best, while his infuriated and blood-thirsty foes glare at him from the opposite side of the threshold, which they dare not cross. Principal Smith takes these pursuing enemies to represent the writer's sins. The spectres of guilt pursue every son of man, for who has not behind him an evil past? But, if a man has taken refuge in God, cast-

ing himself on His mercy, his pursuers dare
not touch him. Undoubtedly this gives a
striking sense to the verse; and the interpretation has this recommendation, that it
still adheres to the pastoral life. But the
author is not so happy in explaining the
sixth verse.

By the perusal of a fascinating booklet,
entitled *The Song of our Syrian Guest,* from
the pen of the Rev. W. A. Knight, the
minds of multitudes on both sides of the
Atlantic have been captured for the view
that the image of shepherd and sheep is con-
tinued to the end of the Psalm. For the
fifth verse this is argued ingeniously, but not
convincingly : the preparing of a table being
taken as the selection of a pasture, the
anointing as the salving of wounds and
bruises, and the cup as the vessel by which
the trough is filled out of which the sheep
drink. Far more natural is the application
of the language to the various features of a
banquet. But it is in the sixth verse that
that interpretation breaks down. A sheep
does not dwell in the " house " of a shep-

herd, unless it be a pet lamb; and this is a condition which does not last "forever." No doubt the word "house" has great latitude of application; and it might possibly refer to the fold, though I do not remember a case where it is so used. When "the house of the Lord" is taken as the palace of the king, in which the banquet of the fifth verse has taken place, the sixth verse is the climax of the whole Psalm, as from its position it ought to be; but under any other interpretation this character is lost.

In short, David is here making use of the experience of the second portion of his own life, as in the image of the shepherd and the sheep he utilises the experience of the first. As in youth he was a shepherd abiding in the fields, in manhood he was a king living in a palace. One of the obligations of a king is to be an entertainer, exercising a frequent and a splendid hospitality. In this virtue, we know from the historical records of his reign, David did not come short; he had the cordiality and the personal fascination by which hospitality is rendered delightful. Many a guest had he made happy at his table, thereby binding him in triple loyalty to his own person ; and, as in his own conduct as a shepherd he had found a fruitful image of what God had done, so does he find in this other *rôle*, played by himself with such distinction, an ampler and more intimate representation of the divine goodness.

2. An Image of Activity.

Why is it that the sacred singer forsakes the image of the shepherd and the sheep, and embraces in his poem this one also? I have already given an external reason in the two periods of David's history ; but there is an internal reason as well : it is that the first image is not sufficient to express the spiritual life in its entirety. Some aspects of it were expressed by this image admirably, but others, no less important, could hardly be expressed at all.

For example, it expressed the passive but not the active side of religion.

The Psalm of Psalms

The relation of the sheep to the shepherd is wholly passive : the sheep is fed, it is led, it is protected ; a sheep does nothing for itself, or next to nothing. And there is a side of religion which corresponds to this : in religion God does everything, and man has nothing to do but passively receive. This is a great truth ; but it is not the whole truth. Religion has an active side as well : it is a battle and a victory. Well was David aware of this : he was a great worker for God, a fighter and a victor ; and this side of his religion is expressed in this next image.

Perhaps this is most distinctly hinted at in the phrase, "in the presence of mine enemies," because this denotes that it is a warrior's feast which is described.

Many of the banquets in David's palace must have been of this type. One of the features of his reign was that, like our own King Arthur with his knights of the Round Table, he collected round himself from all parts of the land the young men of promise and aspiration, and trained them up in valour and usefulness. Their exploits were long remembered by their countrymen with pride and affection. At their head were the three mighties, and after these the thirty; Joab and Abishai, Benaiah and Asahel were names familiar for generations afterwards as household words. These David sent forth to clear the land of enemies and to widen its borders on every hand; and, when they came home to record their triumphs, no doubt he feasted them in the palace, making them feel how much he. rejoiced in their valour and their victories.

3. AN IMAGE OF FRIENDSHIP.

Another element of the spiritual life imperfectly expressed by the image of the sheep and the shepherd, but far more adequately set forth by that of entertainer and guest, is communion.

Between sheep and shepherd there is a strong tie : they understand each other, and may be said to love each other. Yet they are far apart : between a brute and a man

The Psalm of Psalms

there is a great gulf fixed. It may be said that the gulf between man and God is wider still. But this is not the case. The Eighth Psalm boldly declares, in the correct translation of the Revised Version, that man has been made but a little lower than God; and all Scripture unites in declaring that man was made in the image of God. Man is capable of knowing, loving and obeying his Creator, and this is his highest honour. It is, indeed, an infinite condescension on the part of God; but He allows and invites man to a far closer fellowship with Himself than it is possible for a sheep to have with a man; and this was the fact of religion which required to be represented through a new image.

A banquet is a living image of fellowship. To invite a man to be your guest is an expression of respect and affection; and it is an intimation that you wish to know more of him, and to come closer to him. The house is adorned, the table is spread with unusual care, and the viands are chosen to give him pleasure and do him honour. As the feast proceeds, distance and shyness are

The Royal Entertainer

broken down ; the lips are opened, and the heart is opened. The host not only gives his entertainment, but he gives himself ; and the guest gives himself in return.

This is an image of religion. Religion is fellowship with God ; this is its very soul and essence. To be religious is to walk with God. It is to move all day long in an atmosphere warmed and enlightened by His presence. It is to realise Him to be so near that you can appeal to Him in every emergency, seek His aid in every time of need, and in every joy make Him your confidant. It is to see Him everywhere—in the sunshine, in the beauty of hill and dale, in the life of the market-place and the vicissitudes of home. This immensely brightens and intensifies life ; and in this sense all a Christian's life may be said to be a banquet. Others, sitting at the table of Providence, receive ordinary fare ; but those who enjoy God in everything partake of festal food. A crust, if God's blessing is given with it, and if it is received with thankfulness, causes more enjoyment than the most savoury food where God is forgotten. To the mind which can discern God the whole world becomes a king's palace.

But in another sense the Christian life may be compared to a banquet : not only is God in every part of it, but now and then He favours the soul with special seasons of communion. In its very nature a feast is an occasional thing : it does not take place every day. And perhaps, therefore, the experience for which it stands is one which is not the Christian's daily portion, but given as a special favour and reward now and then. There are such seasons : religion has not only its ordinary tenor, but its exceptional experiences—its mounts of transfiguration and its evenings in the upper room. At such times God comes very near, and fellowship is very close. Of such occurrences the saints of every age have spoken. Says one :

Upon my heart, bestowed by Thee,
  More gladness I have found
Than they, even then when corn and wine
  Did most with them abound.

The Royal Entertainer

Another, on the evening of a day spent in communion, said, "I had rather be a doorkeeper in the house of my God than dwell in the tents of wickedness." St. Paul was caught up to the third heavens, and did not know whether he was in the body or out of the body. Read the *Confessions of St. Augustine*, or the *Sermons of St. Bernard*, Bunyan's *Grace Abounding*, or Rutherford's *Letters*, and you will see that the Christian life has what Bunyan calls its "golden hours"; and what makes these golden is the nearness of God and the sense of the divine love. Ordinary humanity no doubt has its rare and memorable moments too : it is a poor life in which there are not some days which shine like gold and diamonds among the wood, hay and stubble of ordinary experience—days so precious that they would not be exchanged for years of commonplace existence — but nothing earthly can lift the human spirit to such heights as the influence of the Spirit of God.

Perhaps I ought to interpret in detail the

different parts of the banquet as they are described in the text—the food, which is no doubt chiefly intended in the opening words, " Thou preparest a table before me " ; then the delightful extravagance of oil, with its cool touch, so grateful in an Eastern climate, and its fragrance, enveloping the senses ; then the drink, so abundant as to overflow the wine-cup. In Christian experience something could easily be found corresponding to each of these ; and those so disposed may exercise their ingenuity in finding it out. But I will not take the trouble ; these are only poetical amplifications of the idea of a right regal banquet. The most important thing is that which underlies them without being expressed. What is the reason why you go to anyone's table when you are invited ? It is not because you will get a better meal than you would at home, though this may be welcome ; it is not for the abundance and the splendour, though you may feel these to be in place : it is friendship which takes you there ; you go to find your friend, not to receive his food ;

The Royal Entertainer

these externals are only preparations and contributions to the true feast. So, in religion, it is God Himself we seek; and the various blessings of salvation are nothing in themselves except as they bring us nigh to Him.

FOREVER

FOREVER

"Surely goodness and mercy shall follow me all the
 days of my life:
And I will dwell in the house of the Lord forever."

ON a celebrated occasion King David, in
thanking God for the singular success which
had marked his life-history, made special
mention of the fact that God had pledged
to him His goodness for a great while to
come: "Then went King David in and sat
before the Lord, and he said, Who am I, O
Lord God, and what is my house, that Thou
hast brought me hitherto? And this was
yet a small thing in Thy sight, O Lord
God; but Thou hast spoken of Thy
servant's house for a great while to come.
And is this the manner of man, O Lord
God?"

The Psalm of Psalms

It is a wonderful mercy to be able not only to remember the past with gratitude, but to contemplate the future with confidence. Mortals are naturally terrified at the future. However bright the past may have been, the dread haunts them that in the future may be hiding some ironical revenge. After the foaming cup of life has been drunk, there may be bitter dregs at the bottom. We cannot tell what a day may bring forth. Only a step in front of every one of us hangs a dark curtain, which we cannot lift. Who knows what may be awaiting us in any of the unknown days of a new year?. It may be some spectre of misfortune, which will turn all our bright life into darkness. So whispers our ignorance.

Nor is the fear of the future always so vague. Some know that it must contain exceptional trials for them. The young man who has just come to the city to push his fortune finds himself confronted with danger at every turn. All the influences which have hitherto supported and en-

couraged him are left behind; he is sur-
rounded with new temptations; the pace of
life is so fast that he has no time to think,
and the numbers and the novelty bewilder
him. He asks anxiously how he is to
survive the trying time, and whether it is
possible to come out with safety and honour
on the other side.

Many who have long survived this initial
stage yet fear the future, and not without
good cause. They have passed the summit
of life, and see before them the downward
slope on what is called the sunless side
of the hill. They must look forward to a
more limited range of activity, to failing
powers and to the infirmities of old age.
Must the sweetness of life, then, be only
a reminiscence of the past? So the world
believes:

> Gather the rosebuds while ye may,
>   Old Time is still a-flying;
> And that same flower which blooms today
>   Tomorrow will be dying.

Such is the philosophy of the world. But is
there a truer philosophy? is there a gospel

The Psalm of Psalms

which can assure us that the best is still in front—that the sun of life is not sinking behind our backs, but rising in the direction to which our faces are turned?

It is this blessed gospel which is embodied in the text. This Twenty-third Psalm, as we have seen, celebrates the past—it is a record of varied past experience—but it also speaks of the future " for a great while to come."

1. THE FUTURE ON THIS SIDE OF DEATH.

The sacred poet does not assume that the future will contain no difficulties or perils for him. On the contrary, he knows that his life is to be one of service and warfare. It is the same person we have speaking in this last verse who, in verse 5, described himself as seated at the table of the king, anointed with oil and drinking an overflowing cup. But, as we saw, that was a warrior, and the banquet was a reward for deeds bravely done. When, however, the feast is over, the soldier must gird on his armour again and return to the field. Enemies have been vanquished, but not the whole of them; there are still battles to fight and victories to win.

If we are in the army of God and know what it is to be rewarded by communion with Himself for past services, we must not grow weary in well-doing. There remains yet very much land to be possessed. God does not call us to a valetudinarian and cloistered virtue. He desires us to perform our part in the struggle of life, and in the common business of the world to play the man for Him. Besides, there is the burden of His cause to be borne, and the means have to be provided for extending His reign. The earth is the Lord's and must not be surrendered to the devil. Every department of human effort is yet to be holiness to the Lord; every corner of the globe is to be filled with His glory; every tribe of the human race to be numbered among His people. Every false form of faith must be exploded; every practice of cruelty and oppression by which the world is cursed must come to an end. The struggle

The Psalm of Psalms

is a long one; it is full of labour and peril;
no Christian, however, dare decline it; to
his dying day he must be a soldier.

But, as he leaves the banqueting house, to
return to the field of action, who are these
two figures that accompany him by order of
the king? "Goodness and Mercy shall
follow me all the days of my life." These
two divine attributes are here personified:
they are servants appointed to follow the
departing guest, to see that no evil befalls
him; they are guardian angels sent to pro-
tect him from calamity. In the Homeric
poems gods and goddesses sometimes descend to the earth and visit the field of
battle, to assist their favourites. In a
moment of deadly peril a goddess will
diffuse round the warrior who is too
severely pressed a mist, in which he is removed from the sight of his foes; or, as-
suming human shape, a god will plunge into
the struggle in which the mortal in whom
he is interested is being worsted and, with
a spear before whose point everything goes
down, completely turn the tide of battle.

Forever

No such mythology finds admission into the sacred Scriptures ; but this is something like the function here intended for the personified Goodness and Mercy.

What attractive figures these two are—how full of sympathy and bounty ! Can there be any misfortune for which divine Goodness cannot find a remedy ? How can life ever become bare and empty when this kind angel is present, ready to pour in strength from the horn of plenty ? Still more welcome is Mercy ; ah, we cannot afford to be without her. Of all the dangers which the future contains, our chief fear is the danger arising from ourselves. The battle, however severe, would be nothing, if only we were absolutely sure of our own loyalty. But we have in us an evil heart of unbelief, which departs from the living God ; the old man within us would betray the whole cause to the enemy ; terrible is the force of besetting sin, frequent are our fits of coldness and backsliding. We require mercy every day.

But goodness and mercy shall follow us

The Psalm of Psalms

all the days of our life. In days of prosperity they will be with us, lest pride
should betray us ; in days of adversity, lest
fear should make us turn back. It is true we
can never tell with what a portent any new
day may be in travail ; but, let it be what it
may, yet, if Goodness and Mercy be with us,
what need we fear ? In the hot days of
youth and in the feeble days of old age ; in
the busy day of action, in the sequestered
day of thought, and in the holiday of repose still they will be with us. As we
sleep, they will keep watch and ward ; and,
when we awake, they will be ready to accompany us. In the day when friends are
many they will be there, the best friends of
all ; and in the day when all have deserted
us they will be there, never leaving or for-
saking us. Finally, on the day of death,
when the world is fading from our grasp,
and around us are crowding the new shapes
of the world unknown, still these old and
familiar figures will be with us—" Goodness
and Mercy shall follow me all the days of
my life."

2. THE FUTURE ON THE OTHER SIDE OF DEATH.

The "great while to come," for which David had received the assurance of the Divine countenance, did not merely reach to the very end of this earthly life but extended beyond the boundary of death—"and I will dwell in the house of the Lord forever."

"The house of the Lord" is a common phrase for the temple or the tabernacle; and many have so understood it here. In this sense the text would mean that David would always have free access to God in His earthly house; and, of course, "forever" might not mean more than as long as he should live.

But "the house of the Lord" is not here intended in an ecclesiastical sense. It is the palace of the Divine King—the same in which the banquet of verse 5 took place. As a reward for his exploits the warrior was admitted once into the palace as a guest; the banquet being over, he had to return again to the field of battle; but he looked forward to a time when, all his battles being finished,

he would be invited back to the palace, not
again to enjoy a banquet lasting only for a
night, but to be a permanent inmate of the
place; as Mephibosheth was fed every day at
King David's table.

The figurative language being stripped
away, this looks as if it were the expression
of an assurance that, after the efforts of the
mortal life are over, those who love God will
dwell forever in communion with Him in
heaven.

To us there is nothing in the least novel in
such an idea; but it is very unusual in the
Old Testament — so unusual that many
scholars would declare that it cannot possibly
be supposed to have a place in one of the
Psalms, especially if this be by David. One
of the most extraordinary features of the Old
Testament is the absence from it of the
scenery of the future world to which in the
New Testament we are accustomed. In the
Books of Moses, for example, when the
punishments are described which will ensue
upon disobedience, all kinds of woes which
can be endured in this world are piled up

in the most appalling numbers, but no mention is made of punishment in a future state of existence; and, in the same way, when the rewards are mentioned which are promised to obedience, all earthly blessings, such as long life, plentiful harvests, political peace and domestic joys, are enumerated, but no mention is made of that which, according to our notions, ought to be most prominent of all—the promise of a reward in heaven after death.

Not that the Hebrews supposed that at death life is extinguished, and that there is no existence beyond. Many things might be adduced to prove that they were quite aware that they would continue to exist. Thus when anyone died, he was said to be " gathered to his fathers "; that is, he went to meet in the other world those who had died before him ; and some passages appear to show not only that there would be recognition there, but that the inhabitants lived in nations and tribes, as they had done in this world. But the extraordinary thing is the quality of the future life as they imagined it.

The Psalm of Psalms

The place where the dead assemble is called Sheol; and they often speak as if it were located somewhere below ground; but there is no clear description of it; and no wonder, for it is "the land of darkness and the shadow of death; a land of darkness, as darkness itself, without any order, and where the light is as darkness." Dim and shadowy, too, is the existence there : " there is no work, nor device, nor knowledge, nor wisdom in Sheol."

In such a prospect there was nothing to attract, but quite the reverse. Accordingly, the way in which even good men speak in the prospect of death is totally unlike what we should now expect in the mouth of a Christian. Read, for example, the prayer of Hezekiah, when he was sick and expected to die. There is not in it a scintillation of any bliss to which he was looking forward on the other side of death. On the contrary, he says, " I shall not see the Lord, even the Lord in the land of the living. Nothingness cannot praise Thee; death cannot celebrate Thee; they that go down into the pit cannot hope for Thy truth." Similarly in Psalm Thirty, a good man in prospect of death, but pleading hard for life, prays, "What profit is there in my blood when I go down to the pit? shall the dust praise Thee? shall it declare Thy truth?" And another psalmist pleads in similar circumstances, "For in death there is no remembrance of Thee; in the grave who shall give Thee thanks?" "The dead praise not the Lord," says another, "neither any that go down into silence." The Ecclesiast is the most doleful of all : "The living know that they must die; but the dead know not anything; neither have they any more a reward; for the memory of them is forgotten. Also their love and their hatred and their envy is now perished; neither have they any more a portion forever in anything that is done under the sun."

What may have been the purpose of God in keeping the secret of the world to come hidden from so many of His servants, is an extremely interesting question. Perhaps it was because He wished them first to recognise that religion is a good thing for this life,

apart altogether from a life to come.
Certainly, when we read how the saints of the
Old Testament rejoiced in God and declared
that His love had made them happier than
the godless ever could be, even when their
corn and wine abounded, and when we re-
flect that these saints perhaps knew little or
nothing about the rewards of the next life,
we begin to suspect that perhaps their
religious standpoint is not lower but higher
than our own. Is our secret feeling not
sometimes that the religious life in this world
is a poor affair, the prizes and tit-bits falling
mostly to the worldly and the wicked, but
that what religion costs here will be compensated by the pleasures of the world to
come? And, if this is our thought, were not
those far above us who, apart altogether from
the punishments and rewards coming afterwards, were confident that wickedness in all
its forms is despicable and detestable, but
that godliness is life and peace?

Another reason why the saints of the Old
Testament were kept in the dark on this
subject may have been that God does not

reveal the truth till it is needed. Truth given to those unprepared for it would have been little prized; but, when they were stretching out their hands and yearning with their whole hearts for it, then the revelation was seized with avidity and retained with tenacity.

In the Old Testament we see the human mind being prepared for the revelation of immortality, till at last it may be said to be panting for it, as the hart for water-brooks.

The need of it was felt in two ways. On the one hand, it was felt to be necessary, in order to make up for the imperfect justice of this life. The Mosaic Law taught that godliness and righteousness would have for reward prosperity in this world; and this was echoed in a hundred forms in the sacred books, as in the First Psalm, "Blessed is the man that walketh not in the counsel of the ungodly, nor standeth in the way of sinners, nor sitteth in the seat of the scornful. But his delight is in the law of the Lord, and in His law doth he meditate day and night. He shall be like a tree planted by the rivers of

The Psalm of Psalms

water, that bringeth forth his fruit in his season; his leaf also shall not wither; and whatsoever he doeth shall prosper." But although this principle, of prosperity attending the steps of the righteous, was amply justified in the general course of history, it was not justified in every case. Sometimes the good man was not prosperous, and sometimes the wicked were. In such cases what was to be said? God's justice was not vindicated in this life; must there not be compensations in another life? Job was an example of calamity after calamity falling on a righteous man, and the whole Book of Job may be said to consist of the moans and cries of the human soul, as it knocked at the gate of God for the revelation of immortality.

But the human spirit was also brought to the same point along a happier path. Life, according to Hebrew ideas, was the breath of God: at the Creation God breathed into man's nostrils the breath of life, and he became a living soul; death, on the other hand, is the withdrawal of the divine breath. But, by living in constant intercourse with

Forever

God, might not the human being be so filled
with the divine energy that he could not die?
Sometimes the saints, when living very near
to God, felt themselves to be so full of health
and strength, derived from God Himself, that
the conviction forced itself on their minds
that nothing, not even temporal death, could
separate them from His love.   This is the
glorious feeling of the Sixteenth Psalm:

I have set the Lord always before me:
Because He is at my right hand, I shall not be
    moved.
Therefore my heart is glad, and my glory rejoiceth:
My flesh also shall dwell in safety.
For Thou wilt not leave my soul to Sheol;
Neither wilt Thou suffer Thine holy one to see
    corruption.
Thou wilt shew me the path of life:
In Thy presence is fulness of joy;
At Thy right hand there are pleasures for evermore.

It was along this sunny path of communion
with God that the singer of the Twenty-third
Psalm also was led to belief; and, although
his vision may have lasted only for a moment,
it would be unwarrantable to deny that he may
have seen the promised land.

The Psalm of Psalms

We, however, are more favourably situated. In the interval between the Old Testament and the New the mists in which the other life was enveloped began to clear away ; and the writers of the New Testament all adopted and developed the faith in immortality. Jesus Himself made the revelation of this hope peculiarly His own. He Himself breathed the atmosphere of the other world ; He raised the dead and was Himself raised from the dead ; He spoke of the many mansions in His Father's house ; and, as we follow His departing figure from the summit of Olivet, we obtain a very near view of that country in which those who have come to Him as the Shepherd and Bishop of their souls will be led to fountains of living water, and those who have worn themselves out in His service on earth will be made to rest from their labours forever.

APPENDIX

APPENDIX

THOUGH I have chosen, for title, THE PSALM OF PSALMS, other phrases may occur to the ingenious. Mr. Meyer has entitled his sweet and tender comment THE SHEPHERD PSALM, and Dr. John Stoughton called his THE SONG OF CHRIST'S FLOCK. A good title by an anonymous author is THE SHEPHERD KING ; and an attractive one might be THE PSALM OF OUR CHILDHOOD.

When occupied with any portion of Scripture, I like to have at hand two commentaries —a thoroughly scientific one, to make clear what exactly the author said and intended, and a more devotional or homiletical one, to suggest applications. For the Psalms, the couple I have thus used most have been Hupfeld and Spurgeon.

Hupfeld is not only the best commentary on the Psalms known to me, but the best com-

Appendix

mentary I have ever used on any part of Scripture. In fact, it taught me what exegesis is. It is rationalistic; but it is easy to discount this; and nothing can surpass its learning and knowledge, its literary appreciation and intellectual grasp. Unfortunately it has not been translated; but much of the essence of it has been transferred to Perowne. Those who prefer what is more recent may turn to Kirkpatrick's three volumes, to be had bound in one, or Briggs' two volumes in the International Commentary.

As for Spurgeon's *Treasury of David*, the bulky volumes and miscellaneous contents will repel scholarly readers. Yet Spurgeon has far more learning than he gets credit for; he seldom misses the drift of a psalm; and in his heaps of accumulations there is many a remark or illustration that can be made to shine like a gem in a discourse. Maclaren's three volumes on the Psalms in the Expositor's Bible are among the best of his expository writings.

INDEX

I. QUOTATIONS

II. TOPICS

THE
SHORT COURSE SERIES

EDITED BY
Rev. JOHN ADAMS, B.D.

This Series is designed to encourage a healthy re-action in the direction of expository preaching. Leading expositors in all the Churches have kindly promised assistance; and the Series, to be issued at the uniform price of 60 cents net per volume, will furnish a sufficiently large variety for individual selection.

NOW READY

A CRY FOR JUSTICE: A Study in Amos.
By Prof. J. E. McFADYEN, D.D., U. F. C. College, Glasgow.

THE BEATITUDES.
By Rev. ROBERT H. FISHER, D.D., Edinburgh.

THE LENTEN PSALMS.
By the Editor.

THE PSALM OF PSALMS.
By Prof. JAMES STALKER, D.D., Aberdeen.

THE SONG AND THE SOIL.
By Prof. W. G. JORDAN, D.D., Kingston, Ontario.

THE HIGHER POWERS OF THE SOUL.
By Rev. GEORGE M'HARDY, D.D., Kirkcaldy.

The Following Other Volumes are in Preparation.

THE STORY OF JOSEPH.
By Rev. ADAM C. WELCH, B.D., Th.D., Glasgow.

SCENES FROM THE LIFE OF DAVID.
By Prof. H. R. MACKINTOSH, D.D., Edinburgh.

A MIRROR OF THE SOUL: Studies in the Psalter.
By Rev. CANON VAUGHAN, M.A., Winchester.

STUDIES IN THE BOOK OF JOB.
By Rev. CHARLES F. AKED, D.D., San Francisco.

THE PROPHECY OF MICAH.
By Principal A. J. TAIT, M.A., Ridley Hall, Cambridge.

THE EXPOSITORY VALUE OF THE REVISED VERSION.
By Prof. G. MILLIGAN, D.D., University of Glasgow.

JEHOVAH-JESUS.
By Rev. THOMAS WHITELAW, D.D., Kilmarnock.

A PREFACE TO THE GOSPEL: An Exposition of Isaiah 55.
By Rev. A SMELLIE, D.D., Carluke.

THE SON OF MAN.
By Prof. ANDREW C. ZENOS, D.D., Chicago.

READINGS IN THE GOSPEL OF ST. LUKE.
By Prof. W. EMERY BARNES, D.D., Cambridge.

THE PARABLE OF THE PRODIGAL SON.
By Principal A. E. GARVIE, D.D., New College, London.

BELIEF AND LIFE: Expositions in the Fourth Gospel.
By Principal W. B. SELBIE, D.D., Mansfield College, Oxford.

THE EMOTIONS OF JESUS.
By Prof. ROBERT LAW, D.D., Toronto.

THE OVERTURES OF JESUS.
By Rev. NEWELL DWIGHT HILLIS, D.D., Brooklyn.

IN THE UPPER ROOM.
By Rev. D. J. BURRILL, D.D., LL.D., New York.

THE "I AM'S" OF OUR LORD.
By Rev. THOMAS MARJORIBANKS, B.D., Edinburgh.

THE SEVEN WORDS FROM THE CROSS.
By Rev. A. B. MACAULAY, M.A., Stirling.

THE PRAYERS OF ST. PAUL.
By Prof. W. G. GRIFFITH THOMAS, D.D., Toronto.

THE METAPHORS OF ST. PAUL.
By Rev. A. BOYD SCOTT, B.D., Glasgow.

THE HOLY SPIRIT.
By Rev. F. STUART-GARDINER, B.D., Kingstown, Ireland.

THE REDEMPTION OF GOD.
By Prof. T. B. KILPATRICK, D.D., Toronto.

STUDIES IN THE APOCALYPSE.
By Prof. W. T. DAVISON, D.D., Richmond.

EXPOSITORY STUDIES.
By Prof. ARTHUR S. PÉAKE, D.D., Manchester.

SOCIAL STUDIES.
By Rev. CANON SIMPSON, M.A., D.D., St. Paul's, London.

OPINIONS OF WEIGHT.

"I thank you very heartily for a copy of your 'Lenten Psalms.' Your 'Short Course Series' finds in this volume an interesting example of the kind of book you are proposing to produce. It is brightly written, and is full of stimulating illustration. I think it exceedingly likely the plan may meet a modern want. The Bible as a backbone for preaching appeals to people better than general sentiment or edifying exhortation of a vague type."

Bishop RYLE, D.D., Dean of Westminster.

"The book is attractive in a high degree, and nothing could be better calculated to stimulate expository preaching in the Churches. One may confidently anticipate for the Series a genuine success."

H. R. MACKINTOSH, D.D., Edinburgh.

"May I express my own judgment that you are working a very fruitful line, and that it will be most acceptable to a great many readers."

J. H. JOWETT, D.D., New York.

"I am wholly with you in this. And I wish you great success in what you are proposing to do. Your plan will help us all to give a scriptural breadth and fulness to our pulpit work. For this and other reasons I hail your proposal, and shall do all that I can to further your good work."

Principal ALEXANDER WHYTE, D.D., Edinburgh.

"You have got hold of a fine idea, and your Series, I am sure, will fulfil a most necessary ministry. There is vast need of just such expository preaching as you wish to encourage."

ALEXANDER SMELLIE, D.D., Carluke.